MW01139619

SPRAYING SKUNKS

by Kristin L. Nelson

Pull Ahead Books

Lerner Publications Company • Minneapolis

This book is available in two editions:
Library binding by Lerner Publications Company, a division of Lerner Publishing Group
Soft cover by First Avenue Editions, an imprint of Lerner Publishing Group
241 First Avenue North
Minneapolis, MN 55401 U.S.A.

Website address: www.lernerbooks.com

Words in *italic* type are explained in a glossary on page 30.

Library of Congress Cataloging-in-Publication Data

Nelson, Kristin L.
    Spraying skunks / by Kristin L. Nelson.
        p.   cm. — (Pull ahead books)
    Summary: Describes the physical characteristics,
behavior, habitat, and life cycle of skunks.
    ISBN: 0–8225–4670–1 (lib. bdg. : alk. paper)
    ISBN: 0–8225–3598–X (pbk. : alk. paper)
    1. Striped skunk—Juvenile literature. [1. Striped
skunk. 2. Skunks.] I. Title. II. Series.
QL737.C25 N45 2003
599.76'8—dc21   2002006591

Manufactured in the United States of America
1 2 3 4 5 6 — JR — 08 07 06 05 04 03

Why is this animal stamping its feet?

This skunk is afraid.
An enemy is near.

The skunk warns its enemy.
HISSSS! The skunk hisses and growls.

Then it raises its tail and arches its back.

Do you know what the skunk does next?

Squirt! The skunk sprays sticky *musk* all over its enemy.

Musk is a smelly yellow liquid.
It sticks to an animal's fur.

A skunk sprayed musk in this
dog's eyes. Ouch—that stings!

Some *predators* are not afraid
of skunks.

Predators are animals that hunt
other animals.
Bobcats hunt skunks.

Great horned owls hunt and eat skunks, too.

What do skunks eat?

Skunks are *omnivores*.
Omnivores eat both plants and
other animals.

This skunk is eating turtle eggs.

Skunks have
long claws
on their
front paws.

Skunks use
their claws
to dig for
food.

These skunks use their sharp claws
to dig up insects and worms.

Sharp teeth help this skunk
nibble on grass.

How does
a skunk
find food
to dig up
and nibble?

Skunks use their small ears to hear insects and other animals.

They use their pointed noses to smell plants and animals.

Skunks are *nocturnal.*
They usually hunt for food at
night and sleep during the day.

Where do skunks sleep?

Skunks sleep in a warm place called a *den*.

Some skunks make their dens inside hollow logs.

Other skunks go underground
to sleep.

Their dens are in holes in
the ground.

Skunks spend most of the
winter in their dens.

They come out to look for food
when it is not too cold.

A skunk's black and white fur
keeps it warm.
But soon the weather will warm up.

What
season
follows
winter?

Spring! A mother skunk gives birth to her babies in the spring.

Baby skunks are called *kittens*. Skunks raise their kittens in dens.

When kittens are born, they have thin fur. The fur is black with white stripes.

Skunks are *mammals*.
They drink their mother's milk.
Milk helps the kittens grow.

The kittens leave the den
with their mother when they are
six weeks old.

The mother skunk protects
her kittens.

The kittens learn to hunt for food and to protect themselves from predators.

This kitten knows how to stamp.

Look out!
These young skunks have
learned to spray.

If you ever see a skunk,
stay away.

It just might
stamp and
spray!

Find your state or province on this map.
Do skunks live near you?

Parts of a Skunk's Body

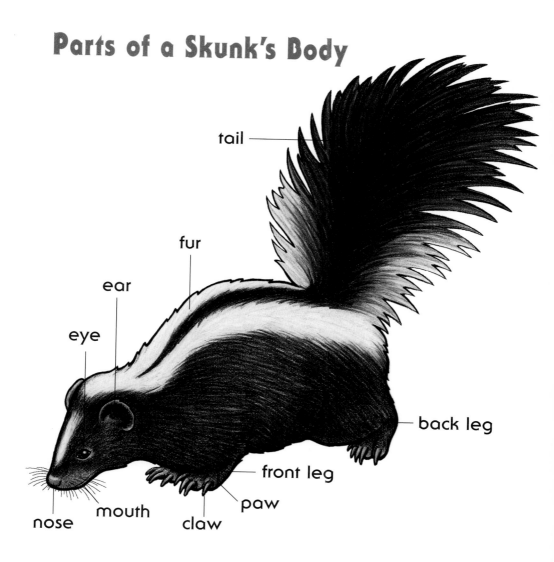

tail

fur

ear

eye

back leg

front leg

paw

nose

mouth

claw

Glossary

den: an animal's home. A den is usually in a hidden area.

kittens: baby skunks

mammals: animals that have fur or hair and drink milk from their mother

musk: a strong-smelling liquid. Skunks spray musk to protect themselves.

nocturnal: active at night

omnivores: animals that eat both plants and other animals

predators: animals that hunt other animals for food

Hunt and Find

About the Author

Kristin L. Nelson loves writing books for children. Along with skunks, she has written books about sharks and raccoons for Lerner's Pull Ahead series. When she is not working on a book, Kristin enjoys reading, walking, and spending time with her son, Ethan, and husband, Bob. She and her family live in Savage, Minnesota.

Photo Acknowledgments

The photographs in this book are reproduced with permission from: © Richard Forbes/Portland State University, pp. 3, 22; © Daniel J. Cox/naturalexposures.com, pp. 4, 11, 16; © Tom Brakefield/CORBIS, p. 5; © Tom & Pat Leeson/Photo Researchers, Inc., p. 6; © David F. Clobes, p. 7; © Robert E. Barber, pp. 8, 9, 23, 26; © Leonard Lee Rue III/Photo Researchers, Inc., p. 10; © Karl Maslowski/Photo Researchers, Inc., p. 12; © Wendy Shattil/Bob Rozinski, pp. 13, 25, 27; © Joe McDonald/Visuals Unlimited, p. 14; © Dwight R. Kuhn, pp. 15, 31; © W. Perry Conway/CORBIS, p. 17; © Renee Lynn/Photo Researchers, Inc., pp. 18, 19; © Jan L. Wassink/Root Resources, pp. 20, 21; © Ed. Cesar/Photo Researchers, Inc., p. 24. Cover Photo: © W. Perry Conway/CORBIS.